TOTALLY AWESOME
Rubber Band Jewelry

Are you ready to make the most awesome, fun accessories EVER?

Then jump into *Totally Awesome Rubber Band Jewelry*, the ultimate companion for making the next big thing for cool kids! With just a few simple tools and easy-to-follow patterns, you can create completely colorful and super stylish bracelets, necklaces, earrings, belts, and other accessories in just minutes. Be pretty in pink with a Back and Forth Bracelet (page 26), hit the pool in style with a Foot Accessory (page 44), and wear your new Fishtail Bracelet (page 20) to the mall. There are so many cool things to make! All you need is a hook (a crochet hook will do), small rubber bands in all the colors you love, small plastic clips to connect your links, and a loom such as Rainbow Loom®, Cra-Z-Loom™, or FunLoom™ to bring it all together. So what are you waiting for? Get looping!

Look What You Can Make!

Learn the Basics

Projects

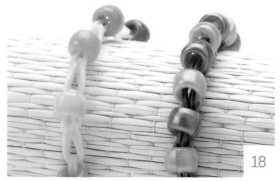

18

Basic Bracelet with Beads

20

Fishtail Bracelet

22

Triple the Fun Bracelet

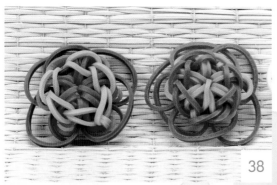

BFF

idea gallery

There is so much you can make with rubber bands and a loom! From necklaces, rings, and accessories to color stacking and adding beads and charms, here are just a few ideas to show you how versatile and fun making your own rubber band jewelry can be!

Make a Ring

Rings are a super easy bonus accessory to make! Just make any bracelet pattern short enough to fit around your finger. Make rings to match all your bracelets!

Design a Necklace

Try making a posh necklace by connecting several strands of basic links! This nifty necklace uses three colorful strands for a pretty, layered look.

Awesome Anklets

Any bracelet can be made into an anklet! Super stretchy basic bracelets will slip right onto your ankle and feel really comfy.

Best Buds

You can make awesome matching sets of bracelets with your best friends at birthday parties, sleepovers, school, or just as special gifts to share.

Show School Spirit

Rubber band jewelry is a quick and easy way to show off at a pep rally! Make a variety of bracelets in your school's colors. You may even get away with wearing them to gym class!

High Fashion

Several bracelets in the same design but different colors make a statement. And throw in a complementary pair of earrings for a full-on rubber band look!

Make a cute collar for a stuffed animal!

Add charms to bracelets and combine similar colors!

Stack a bunch of bracelets for a funky look!

Learn the Basics

Tools and Materials

To get started, you'll need just four simple items, most of which are available at your local craft or toy store. You'll need:

> A loom for rubber band jewelry (such as Rainbow Loom®, Cra-Z-Loom™, or FunLoom™)
> Small plastic clips (C or S clips are best)
> Rubber bands (½" to ¾" in diameter)
> A small crochet hook

Looms can be purchased as kits that include all four items listed above. That's an easy way to start! When you run out of rubber bands (which is sure to happen fast!) or if you want more colors, you can scoot over to your local craft store and buy more in a rainbow of colors. Any craft store that carries the looms will carry the rubber bands and plastic clips—and you'll run out of those, too!

Different looms have different numbers of rows or columns. All the projects and diagrams in this book use the Rainbow Loom®, but don't worry if you have a different loom. As long as you follow the diagrams and instructions exactly, your piece will turn out great. You will just have unused rows or columns of pegs that you can ignore.

Here's a hint: if you have a loom but no hook, it's a good idea to take the loom with you when you buy or borrow a crochet hook. You'll want to pick the size that fits perfectly into your loom! (Size G, 4.25mm, will work well.) See if your grandma or one of your mom's family friends is into crochet, and borrow one of their hooks!

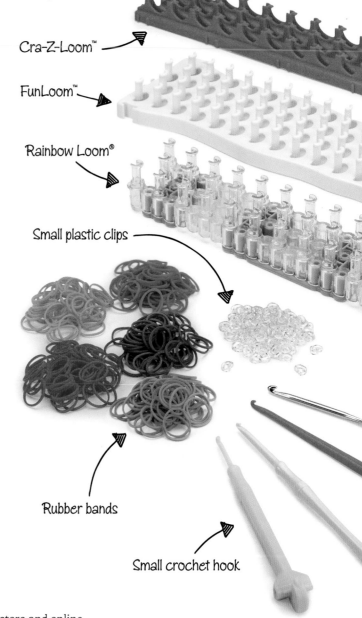

Cra-Z-Loom™

FunLoom™

Rainbow Loom®

Small plastic clips

Rubber bands

Small crochet hook

Here are just some of the colors you can use to make rubber band jewelry!

Keep an eye out for the latest and coolest colors at your local craft store and online.

Shown here are: Fuchsia, Pink, Red, Orange, Caramel, Neon Orange, Yellow, Jelly Yellow, Neon Green, Lime Green, Olive Green, Dark Green, Teal, Turquoise, Jelly Teal, Ocean Blue, Navy Blue, Jelly Blue, Purple, Jelly Purple, Gray, Burgundy, Black, White, Glow in the Dark.

Making the Basic Bracelet on a Loom

This most basic bracelet introduces you to the loom and the general idea of placing bands and looping them. Once you get the hang of it, you'll be making tons of awesome bracelets in just minutes! Check out the helpful diagram on page 13 as you follow these step-by-step instructions.

What You'll Need

> 25 rubber bands (for this example, 13 purple and 12 pink)
> 1 clip
> Loom
> Hook

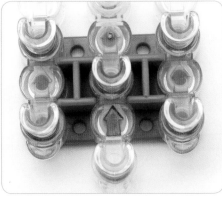

1 Turn your loom so that the arrow faces **up** (away from you); the bottom peg sticks out at the bottom.

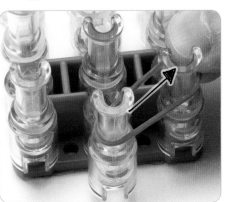

2 Place your first rubber band on the bottom middle peg (the one closest to you) and stretch it onto the bottom right peg.

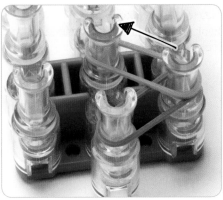

3 Place your second rubber band on the peg you just ended on and stretch it onto the peg to the upper left (the middle peg second from the bottom).

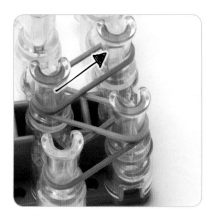

4 Place your third rubber band on the peg you just ended on and stretch it onto the peg to the upper right of it.

5 Keep on repeating this back-and-forth pattern until you've run out of bands or reached the top of the loom. **Always remember to start on the last peg you ended on.**

6 Now you are ready to loop! First, turn your loom so that the arrow at the top is facing **down** (towards you).

7 Starting at the bottom of the loom (closest to you), **push your hook down into the big loop** created by the last band you placed. Hook the second-to-last band you placed, being sure to hook it **inside the groove** on the peg.

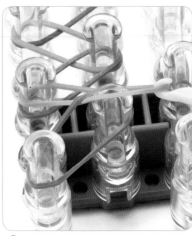

8 Lift the band off the bottom middle peg…

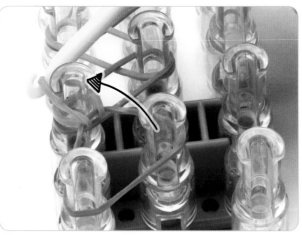

9 …and loop it around the peg to the upper left, which is the other peg that the band is also looped on. This is looping a band back to the peg it came from.

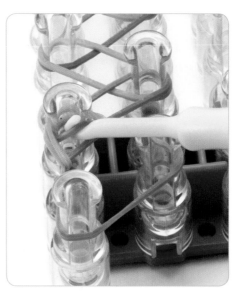

10 Now, push your hook down into the groove in the peg you just looped onto, and hook the next rubber band. Don't hook the one you just looped!

NEVER DO THIS!
Never hook a band by going around the outside as shown in this photo. **ALWAYS** push your hook down into the groove of the peg you are on, down inside the bands that are already looped there, as shown in step 10.

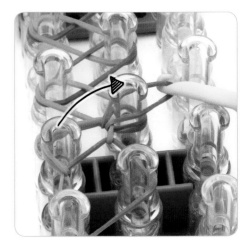

11 Lift the band off the peg and loop it back to the peg it came from.

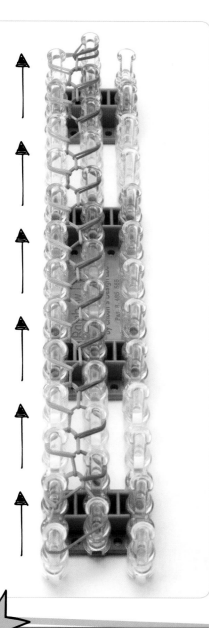

12 Keep on repeating this pattern all the way up to the top of the loom. **Always remember to push your hook down into the groove before hooking the next band.** Here's what your loom should look like after you finish all the looping! Stick with it; soon it'll become like second nature!

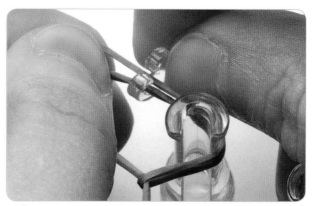

13 Take your clip and hook it around **both strands** of the one rubber band that is looped on the top middle peg, the very last band that you looped. It helps to pull the strands taut with one finger.

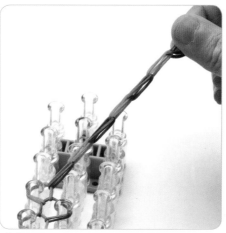

14 Holding the clip firmly between your fingers, pull the bracelet off the loom, one peg at a time. Don't be afraid to pull hard; it won't break!

15 Clip the rubber band on the other end onto the clip. You've made your first bracelet!

CRAFTY TIP!
Colors Galore

You can get creative with color on the very first bracelet you make! The order of your bracelet colors will match the order you place the rubber bands on the loom. If you alternate colors, you'll have an alternating bracelet; if you do three of one color at a time, you'll have stripes along your bracelet! Try laying out your 25 rubber bands in the pattern you want to see.

Try A Different Ending: Little Loop

If you don't like the big loop of the final band on your bracelet, there's an alternative way to finish it off. It's a little tricky, but worth it! Start making another bracelet on your loom, and then, after step 5 (page 9), make this small change. (Note: This will make the bracelet a little bit tighter.)

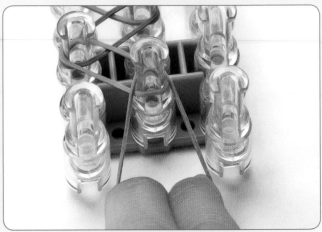

1 Turn the loom so the arrow faces down. Lift the band off of the last peg with two fingers as shown, keeping it looped to the next-to-last peg.

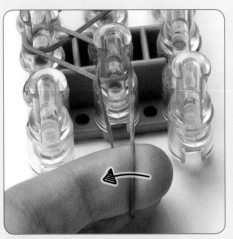

2 Twist your fingers to the left so that the left side of the band goes to the bottom and the right side of the band goes to the top. Hold the loom steady with your free hand.

3 Wrap both strands of the band around the bottom left peg…

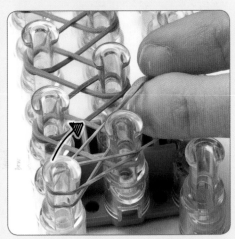

4 … keep wrapping it around, and loop it onto the bottom middle peg. You may want to press against the top of the bottom left peg with a finger to make sure the band doesn't slip off.

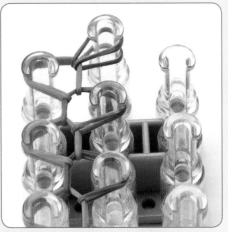

5 Follow the regular directions for steps 7–12 (pages 10–11) to loop the whole loom. Make sure when you start looping that you **dig your hook into the groove** inside the loops on the last peg—don't go around the outside!

6 Clip the two strands of the band on the top middle peg together.

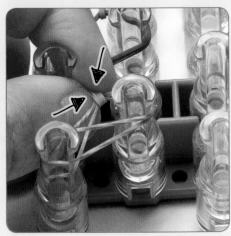

7 Firmly pinch the bands between the second-from-bottom left peg and the bottom middle peg, as shown. Then pull the entire bracelet off the loom, keeping your pinch firm.

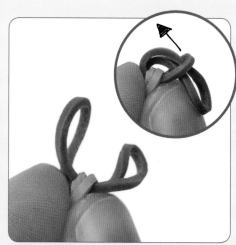

8 Without relaxing your pinch, tug the large loop that is stuck through the small loop free, so that you have two free loops. Even them out.

9 Clip the two loops onto the clip you used at the top of the loom. Now you have a cool symmetrical closure!

Understanding Patterns

Now that you've made a basic bracelet, let's look at the pattern for the basic bracelet so that you will be able to use the patterns in this book. For most projects, there is a **Load It Up!** pattern that you must follow in order to get your bracelet or other project started. This is called loading it or placing it on the loom. Then, you simply follow the step-by-step **Get Loopin'** instructions to make your bracelet. It's that easy!

The **Load It Up!** pattern shows you the order in which you must place your rubber bands and how your loom will look once you have finished placing all your bands. Each pattern shows a specific color arrangement; you can always change the colors, but never change the order!

Load It Up!

Take a look at this **Load It Up!** pattern for the basic bracelet. If you followed the step-by-step directions on page 9, then you followed this pattern the whole way through! Try making another basic bracelet by starting with this pattern, and see if you succeed!

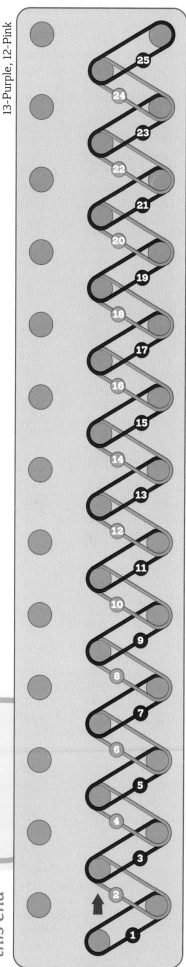

13-Purple, 12-Pink

Start at this end

Making the Basic Bracelet on a Hook

You can also make a basic bracelet without the loom—all you need is a hook! Using this method, you can extend the basic bracelet to be as long as you want—even one hundred links long or longer! This skill will come in handy later when you want to make fun pieces like Hand and Foot Accessories (page 44) and the Hippie Belt (page 46). So give it a try!

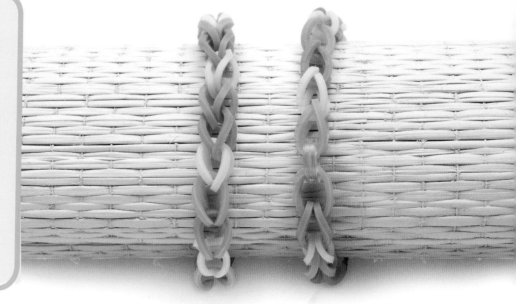

What You'll Need

 9 Neon green bands

 8 White bands

 8 Pink bands

 1 Clip

 1 Hook

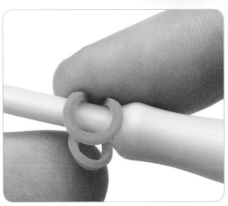

1 To start the bracelet, first fold one band over your hook as shown.

2 Clip the two loops to secure the band around your hook.

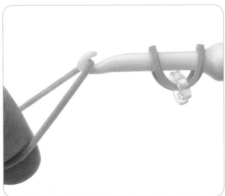

3 Hook your second band onto the tip of the hook, holding it slightly taut with one finger.

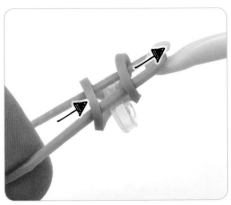

4 Carefully pull the hook, with one end of the second rubber band, all the way back through the double loop, holding onto the other end of the band with your fingers. Don't pull the end you're holding through the double loop.

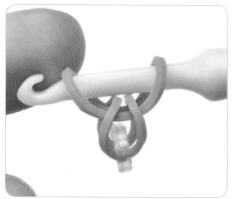

5 Loop the part of the band you are still holding up onto the hook. Make sure the band isn't twisted. The first band will end up underneath the hook.

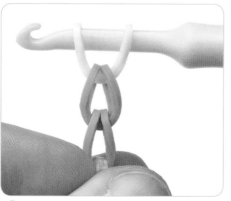

6 Repeat steps 3–5. Be sure to pull one end of the band all the way through both loops formed by the second rubber band.

7 Now, add a battery, pen cap, or other similar small object to the first rubber band loop you made and clipped. This will help weigh it down for the rest of the bracelet! It will make the process much faster.

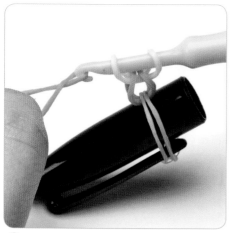

8 Repeat steps 3–5 again, but this time rotate your hook so that the hook faces downwards before you pull it back through the band on the hook. This lets it slide through super easily because of the weight on the bottom that pulls the bands down!

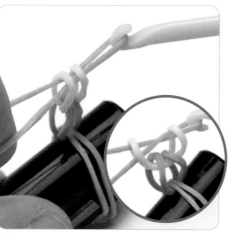

9 Rotate the hook back up before you loop the end of the band you are holding onto the hook. Always make sure the band isn't twisted before you loop the end you're holding onto the hook.

10 Now just continue making links! You can make as many links as you like this way. To make a bracelet, you only need to use about 25 bands.

11 To finish, first remove the weight you added to the beginning of the bracelet.

12 Slide both strands of the last rubber band you looped off the hook and onto two fingers.

13 Keeping the strands taut, slide both of the strands on your fingers onto the clip you used to start the bracelet. Finished! You've made a basic bracelet without using the loom!

Terrific Tips and Tricks

Making Slip Knots

Several more complicated bracelets in this book require slip knots to secure them because of the number of bands at one end of the bracelet. You can't shove six or eight bands into one clip very easily! Here's how to make this simple but strong knot. In the example shown, you are completing a bracelet that has a whopping six strands at the top that you'll need to connect. Come back and read this section once you've started to make a bracelet that requires a slip knot (like the Triple the Fun Bracelet, page 22).

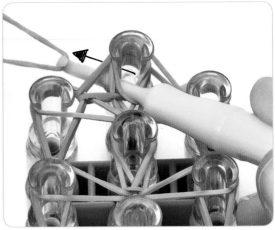

1 Dig your hook down into the groove of the last peg. Grab a new band (a finishing band) and hook it onto the hook at the base of the peg where the hook comes out, as shown. Slide the other end of the band securely around your finger.

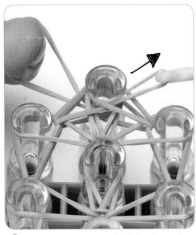

2 Pull the hook end of the band all the way up through the peg, being careful not to snag the other rubber band strands.

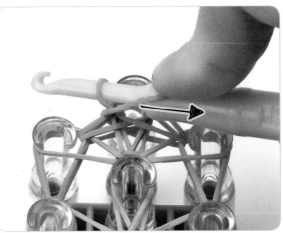

3 Loop the band on your finger onto the hook, placing it **behind** the band that's already there. Hold it down against the hook with one finger so that it doesn't get mixed up with the other loop.

4 Grab the front loop—the one that is closest to the hook end of the hook—and slide it onto one finger…

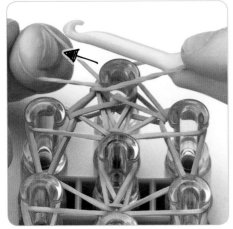

5 …then pull it off the hook, keeping it on your finger.

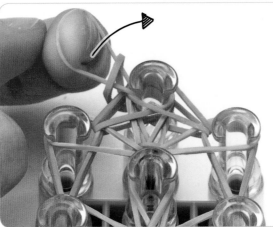

6 Now slide the remaining loop off the hook, and start to pull the loop on your finger to tighten the knot. As you pull, slide the knot around to the very top of the peg to center the knot.

Adding Links for Length

Sometimes, because of the way different rubber band bracelets are looped together, they don't have as much stretch and won't fit your wrist. If you come up short, you have two options: you can either make the bracelet longer by combining two looms (see below), or you can simply add basic links—the same ones used to make the basic bracelet on the hook (pages 14–15)—to extend the bracelet. Because most of us don't have two looms, adding basic links is the solution—and it's super easy! Here's how.

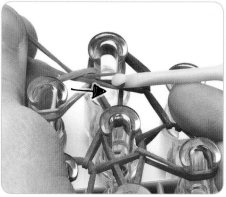

1 Start off as if you are making a slip knot by pulling a band up through the final peg or set of bands (Making Slip Knots, steps 1–2).

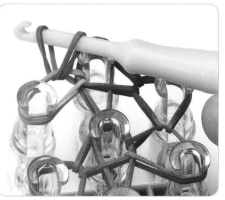

2 Loop the band you're holding onto the hook, but don't cross it over the loop already on the hook—place it in front of the band that's already there, instead of behind it like you do for a slip knot.

3 Now start making basic links just like you did when making the basic bracelet on a hook (pages 14–15)! Hook another band…

4 …twist and pull one end through…

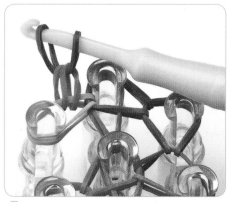

5 …and loop the other end onto the hook.

6 Now you can extend any of your bracelets to the perfect size, no matter what the bracelet design is!

CRAFTY TIP!
Combining Looms

If you want to make a long necklace, a big bracelet, or any other longer piece of jewelry with your rubber bands, you can usually buy more than one loom and then connect them end-to-end. You can double the length of your accessory that way!

Basic Bracelet with Beads

Adding snazzy beads to the basic bracelet will really funk it up! Here you'll learn how to add beads in an every-other pattern, but you can add as many or as few beads as you like. Experiment!

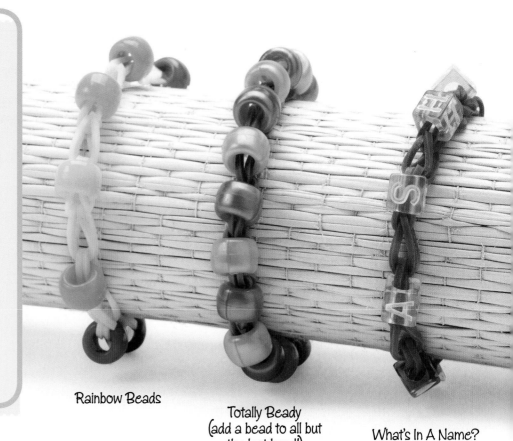

Rainbow Beads

Totally Beady
(add a bead to all but the last band!)

What's In A Name?

What You'll Need

17
White bands

1
Clip

8
Pony beads

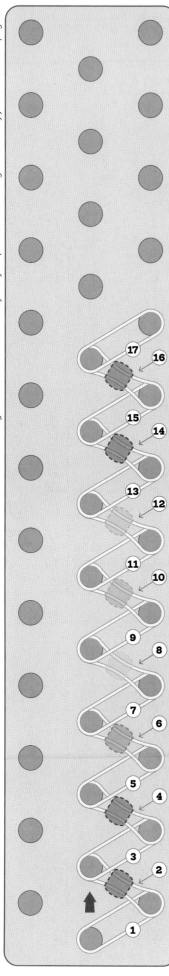

Start at this end

Load It Up!

Place rubber bands on the loom the same way as when you are making a basic bracelet on a loom (page 9). But slide a pony bead onto every other band before placing it on the loom, as shown in the pattern. Don't put a pony bead on the first or last band. If you are spelling a word using every other band (bands 2, 4, 6, etc.), make each letter bead upside down, with the letters facing to the upper right instead of the lower left, or your word will end up backwards!

Get Loopin'

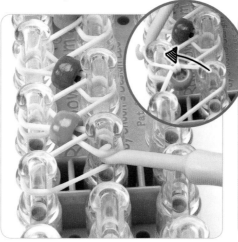

1 Turn the loom so the arrow faces down, then start looping bands just as you do for the basic bracelet. Start with the last band with a pony bead on it—**hook it from inside** the last white band you placed.

2 Loop the next band, but be sure to **push your hook down into the groove** and inside both the loops formed by the bead band you just looped. The bead will try to get in the way; you will probably have to pull it down with your fingers to see what you are doing.

3 Try looking at the loom from the side, too, to make sure you've hooked the right band.

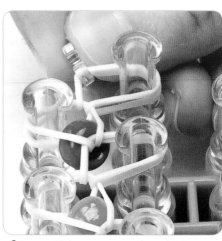

4 Loop all the remaining bands this way, add a clip to the top, and pull the bracelet off your loom.

Fishtail Bracelet

This easy-as-pie bracelet only uses two pegs and one simple pattern, but the effect is really cool! Try stripes of different widths by using two, three, or more of the same color in a row. If you want to include beads, as in Fishy Pony Beads, just slide a bead onto a band before adding it to the loom. Try putting four or five bands between each band with a bead.

Cotton Candy

Bumblebee

Fishy Pony Beads

What You'll Need

○ **18** Pink bands

○ **15** Turquoise bands

○ **15** White bands

○ **2** Extra bands (any color)

⊙ **1** Clip

1 First place one rubber band in a figure eight shape around two pegs that are next to each other. Make sure the peg grooves face to the right, so the arrow on the loom faces to the right.

2 Place two more bands, one at a time, on the same two pegs, without twisting them into figure eights.

3 Hook the bottom band to the left of where it crosses for the figure eight.

4 Loop it up and off the peg it's looped on, letting it go in the center.

5 Do the same with the bottom band to the right side, looping it off the peg it's looped on.

6 Now the bottom band is securely looped around the other two bands.

7 Add another band to the two pegs, without twisting it.

8 Unloop the new bottom band as you did for the first band, one side at a time.

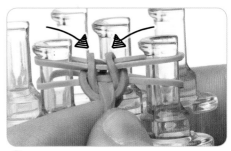

9 Add another band, and then unloop the new bottom band. Repeat this for all your bands, or until you reach the desired length. As you go, tug on the base of the bracelet.

10 Don't forget to use your two extra bands as the last bands you place. Then, hook a clip onto the last band you unlooped, making sure to hook both strands of the band.

11 Bring the other end of the bracelet around to hook both strands of the first band to the clip, too.

12 Slide the bracelet off the pegs and pull the two final loose bands out.

Triple the Fun Bracelet

This bracelet is easy to make in rows of stripes or chevrons. For a more muted look, try making the horizontal base bands many colors and the vertical colored bands all one color. Plus, it fits nice and flat on your wrist so you don't have to worry about it twisting around!

Cool Color Blocks

Peekaboo Rainbow

Chic Chevron

What You'll Need

12 Turquoise bands

12 Neon green bands

12 Purple bands

12 White bands (base bands)

1 White finishing band

1 Clip

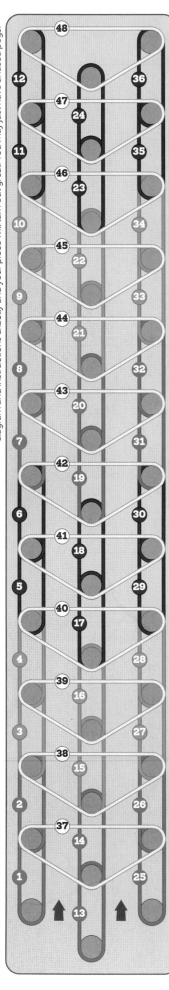

Start at this end

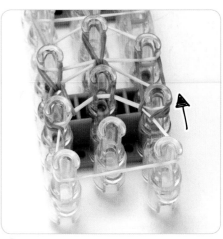

Load It Up!

Place rubber bands up each of the three columns, one column at a time. Then, place the base rubber bands around each set of three pegs as shown, forming triangles. Remember to skip the bottom set of three!

Get Loopin'

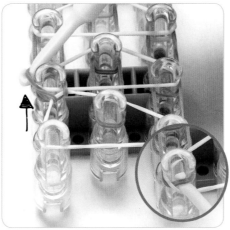

1 Turn the loom so the arrow faces down. First, hook the bottom left colored band **up through** the white band and loop it onto the peg immediately above it. Make sure you pull it up through the white band as shown (inset)!

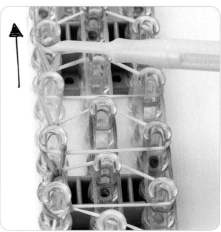

2 Loop the entire left column the same way as you did the first band in step 1, making sure to pull each band up through the white bands, **not around the outside** of the white bands.

3 Next, starting with the bottom middle colored band, loop the entire middle column the same way.

4 Then, loop the entire right column the same way. Make sure you pull the bands **up through** the white bands, not outside them!

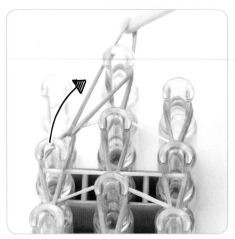

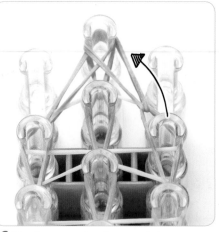

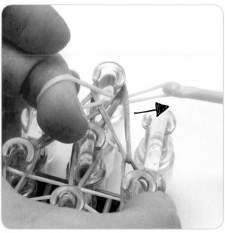

5 At the very top of the loom, hook the two strands off the top left peg and loop them onto the top middle peg.

6 Do the same for the top right, hooking both bands from the top right peg and looping them onto the top middle peg. Now you have six strands of band on the top middle peg.

7 Now, make a slip knot (see page 16) with the finishing band around all the rubber bands on the top middle peg.

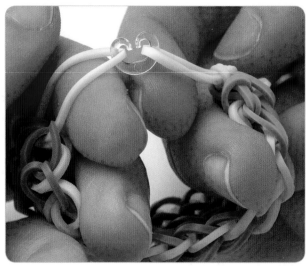

9 Attach the two end rubber bands with a clip. You're ready for triple the fun!

8 It's time to pull your bracelet off the loom!

CRAFTY TIP!

Clips and Jump Rings

The plastic clips made for rubber band jewelry generally work quite well. But if you're having trouble getting your bracelets to stay together, or if you just want to be extra sure that your bracelets last forever, you can use jump rings bought at your local craft store instead. They're trickier to work with—you'll probably need two small sets of pliers to open and close the rings—but they are a super-secure alternative for making sure your jewelry creations shine day after day!

37-White (includes finishing band), 1-Neon Orange, 1-Yellow, 1-Red, 1-Fuchsia, 1-Pink, 1-Purple, 1-Turquoise, 1-Ocean Blue, 1-Navy Blue, 1-Dark Green, 1-Lime Green, 1-Neon Green

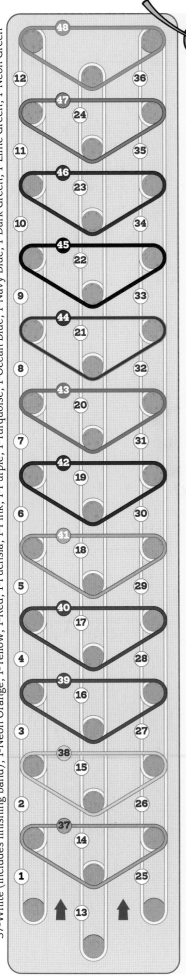

Peekaboo Rainbow: This design turns your bracelet into a pretty surprise! Look closely, and you'll see your rainbow. This design isn't hard at all. White and black both work great as contrasting colors for the rainbow to shine through.

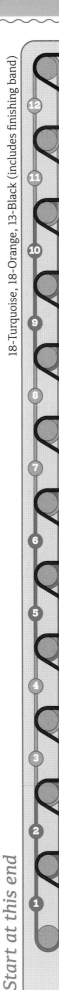

18-Turquoise, 18-Orange, 13-Black (includes finishing band)

Chic Chevron: If stripes just aren't your thing, try this design! You just sandwich every other row of colors, alternating colors, as shown in the pattern. The effect is a cool chevron design that adds pep and movement to an already stylish accessory.

Back and Forth Bracelet

How fun is this multicolored bracelet? Jump back and forth between colors in whatever pattern you like. Mix and match! The looping for this bracelet is a bit tricky, but if you pay close attention, you're sure to make the coolest bracelet ever!

Roses in Bloom

Grass Green and Sky Blue

School Spirit

What You'll Need

 **17** Pink bands

17 Fuchsia bands

16 Red bands

1 Clip

Start at this end

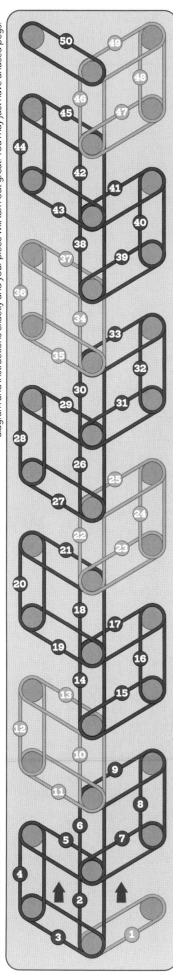

Load It Up!

First, place a starter band at the bottom of the loom. Then place a set of four bands of one color in the order shown (bands 2–5). Then, in your second color, place another set of four, but on the other side of the loom as shown (bands 6–9). Then, place your third color in the same way, on the other side. Keep making these tilted squares to the end, and add one last band.

Before You Begin...

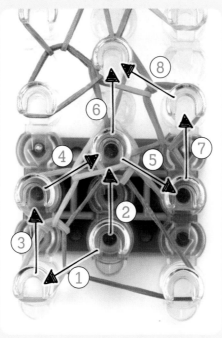

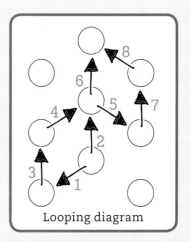

Looping diagram

Looping this bracelet is easy once you understand the looping pattern. It's done in squares of 4, once to the left, once to the right, for a total pattern of 8 loops. Take a look at this diagram before you begin, then go ahead and start looping with step 1!

Get Loopin'

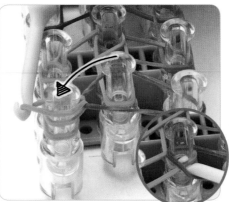

1 Turn the loom so the arrow faces down. **Loop** ①: Hook the top pink band from the bottom middle peg, and loop it onto the bottom left peg, the peg it came from.

2 Loop ②: Hook the remaining pink band on the same peg you just looped from, and loop it onto the peg directly above it. Again, this is looping it onto the peg it came from.

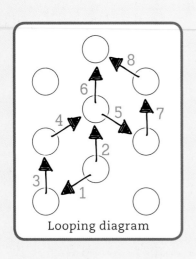

Looping diagram

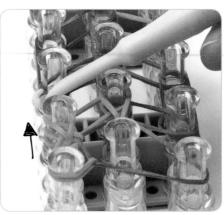

3 Loop ③: Hook the bottom pink band from the bottom left peg, and loop it onto the peg directly above it. Make sure you **push your hook down into the groove** to hook it.

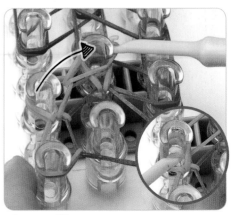

4 Loop ④: Hook the bottom pink band from the peg you just ended on, and loop it onto the peg to the upper right of it. This completes one square of color!

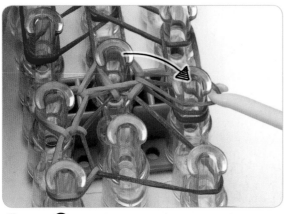

5 Loop ⑤: Now for the second square of color. First, hook the top red band on the last peg you looped to, and loop it to the peg to the bottom right of it (which is the peg that it came from. Don't forget to push your hook down into the groove to hook the band!

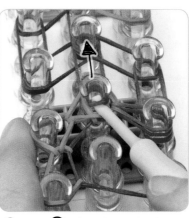

6 Loop ⑥: Then, loop the remaining red band on the same peg you just looped from to the peg directly above it.

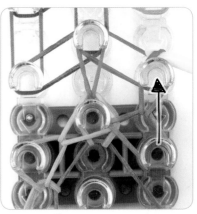

7 Loop ⑦: Now hook the bottom red band on the side, and loop it onto the peg directly above it.

8 Loop ⑧: Finally, hook the bottom red band from the peg you just ended on, and loop it onto the peg to the upper left of it. This completes the second square of color! Now repeat this pattern of 4 loops on the lefthand squares and 4 loops on the righthand squares for the rest of the bracelet. Follow the diagram!

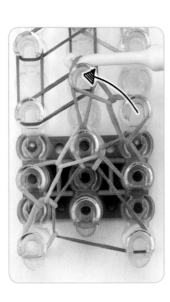

9 Loop the last band from the top middle peg to the top left peg.

10 Add extra links if you want to (see page 17). Add a clip to the last link you made, and pull the bracelet off the loom.

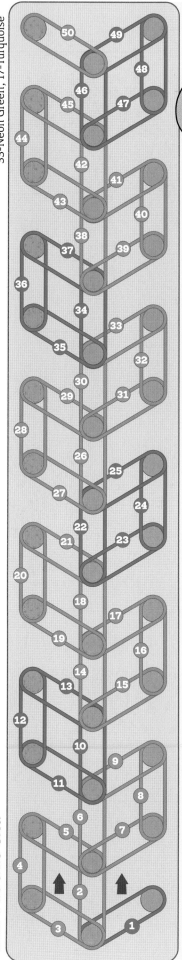

Start at this end

Start at this end

Grass Green and Sky Blue: To make this pretty nature-inspired design, alternate two green squares with one blue square. You'll be longing for a walk in the park!

School Spirit: For a bold bracelet that shouts out your scholastic pride, alternate every square with your school's colors. You'll be the snazziest student at the pep rally!

Zipper Bracelet

This zipper might not be functional, but it sure is stylish! You can make the zipper all one color, mix up the background colors, alternate colors... do whatever you want! And there's a secret to this bracelet... if you turn it "inside out" on your wrist, you get a totally different bonus bracelet (below)! How cool is that?

Tropical

Royalty

Zip the Rainbow

What You'll Need

25 Pink bands

10 Turquoise bands

10 Neon orange bands

1 Pink finishing band

1 Clip

Start at this end

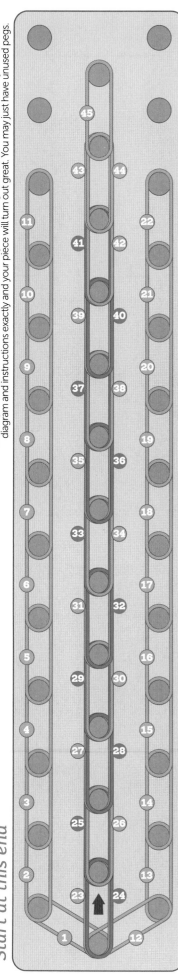

Load It Up!

First, place all the bands on the two outer columns according to the order shown. Stop with two empty pegs at the top. Then, place bands up the center column—but the trick here is you're placing **two** on each pair of pegs! Place one at a time so that they don't get twisted together. To make the cool alternating blue and orange of this bracelet, alternate which you place first in each pair: for the first set, place orange, then blue; for the second set, place blue, then orange. Finish with pink bands 43–45.

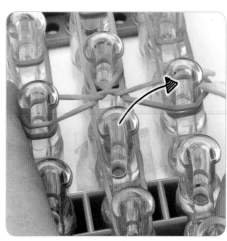

Get Loopin'

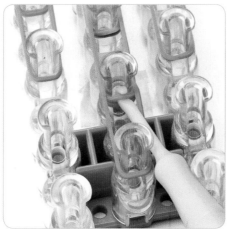

1 Turn the loom so the arrow faces down. First, hook the top band (pink) on the second-from-bottom middle peg, making sure the bands aren't crossed.

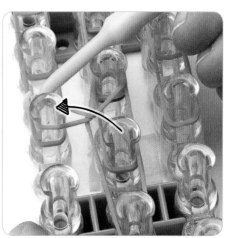

2 Loop the band to the peg to the upper left of it.

3 Hook the remaining band on the peg you just looped from.

4 Loop the band to the peg to the upper right of it.

5 Hook the bottom band on the bottom left peg, making sure you go **down into the groove** to hook it, not around the outside.

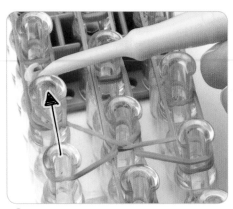

6 Loop the band to the peg immediately above it.

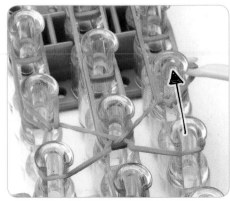

7 Hook and loop the bottom band on the bottom right peg and loop it to the peg above it as you did in steps 5–6.

8 Push your hook **into the groove** of the third-from-bottom middle peg and hook the top band (neon orange).

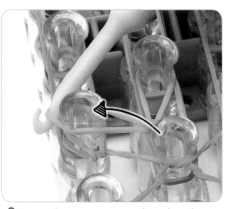

9 Loop the neon orange band to the peg to the upper left of it.

10 Hook the bottom band (turquoise) from the peg you just looped from, and loop it to the peg to the upper right of it, as you did in steps 8–9. Make sure you **hook from the center of the groove; DO NOT** go around the outside of the other bands!

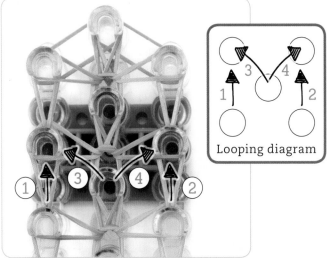

Looping diagram

11 Repeat the pattern for the rest of the bracelet: first loop the bottom band up on the left column, then up on the right column; then loop the top band from the middle peg to the upper left, then the bottom band from the middle peg to the upper right. **When looping ③ and ④, ③ is always the top band and ④ is always the bottom band,** though the colors may change.

12 Loop the bottom band (pink) from the top left peg to the top middle peg, and do the same on the right side.

13 Secure the bands on the top peg with a slip knot (see page 16); you may want to extend the bracelet length with extra links (page 17). Pull the bracelet off the loom.

26-Purple (includes finishing band), 20-Yellow

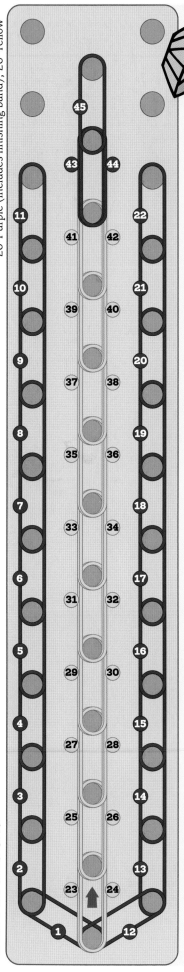

Royalty: You'll feel like a real queen in these royal colors! The Royalty bracelet uses just yellow and purple, with all one color on the zipper. Pay close attention while you're looping so that you hook the right yellow band every time!

26-White (includes finishing band), 2-Yellow, 2-Neon Orange, 2-Red, 2-Fuchsia, 2-Pink, 2-Lime Green, 2-Teal, 2-Turquoise, 2-Navy Blue, 2-Purple

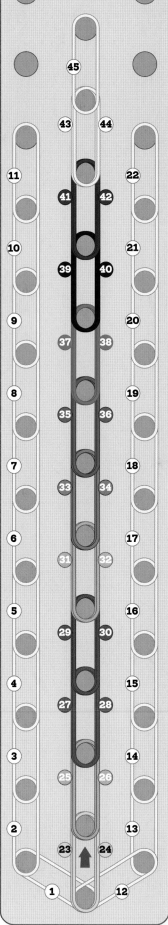

Zip the Rainbow: Rainbows make great zippers, and the proof is right here! A white background makes the zipper really pop.

Totally Awesome Rubber Band Jewelry **33**

Starburst Bracelet

This bracelet will really put your looping skills to work! First learn to make the bracelet by making the Multicolor Stars variation, because it will be a lot easier to keep track of what you're doing with the different colors. Once you've got the hang of it, you can try making all sorts of cool patterns!

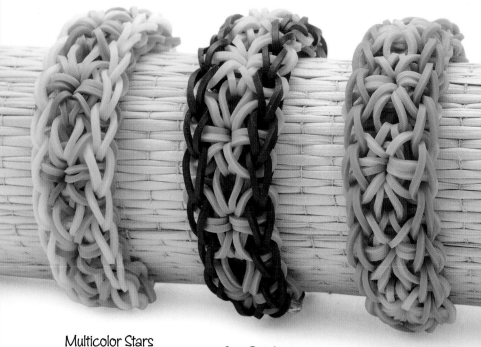

Multicolor Stars

Star Rainbow

Pretty Peonies

What You'll Need

- ◯ **33** White bands
- ◯ **6** Red bands
- ◯ **6** Neon orange bands
- ◯ **6** Yellow bands
- ◯ **6** Lime green bands
- ◯ **6** Turquoise bands
- ◯ **6** Purple bands
- ◯ **1** White finishing band
- ◯ **1** Clip

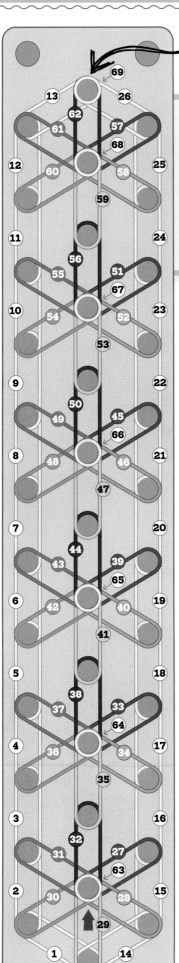

Start at this end

Look!

Load It Up!

Loading this loom is pretty easy. Place a starting band at the bottom, load up the left column, then load up the right column. Then, create the starbursts with six bands each. Make sure you go in exactly the order shown. *The last step is to add one double-looped band to the single peg in the center of each of the six starbursts; then add one to the top middle peg as well (bands 63–69).* There's nothing tricky about this: just loop the band onto the peg and then loop it on again, as if you're tying your ponytail with a hair elastic.

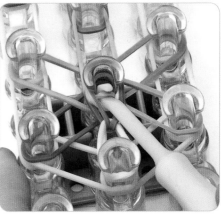

Get Loopin'

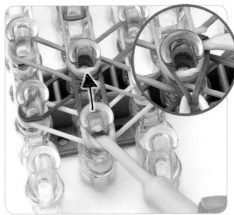

1 Turn the loom so the arrow faces down. Push your hook **down into the groove** of the bottom middle peg, and hook the first band beneath the double-looped band (in this bracelet it is purple). Loop the band to the peg directly above it.

2 Next, push your hook **down into the groove** of the center of the first starburst. Hook the band that is stretched from the center of the starburst down to the right. (In this bracelet, it's turquoise.) Make sure you push your hook down through the white double-looped band.

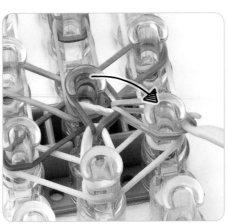

3 Loop the band you hooked to the peg to the bottom right, the peg it came from. This first band is the hardest to get right in each starburst.

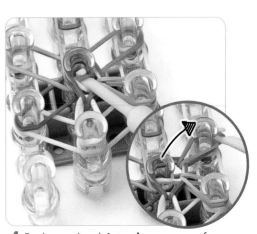

4 Push your hook **into the groove** of the center peg of the starburst and hook the next band down, which is the one that is stretched from the center of the starburst up to the right. Loop it to the peg to the upper right.

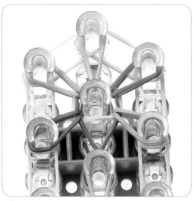

5 Move counterclockwise and loop the remaining bands in the starburst—there are three more—the same way you looped the first two. When you are done, you should have a big loop around the middle peg, as shown.

6 Here is the looping diagram to follow for each of the remaining five starbursts. Start by looping the bottom band of the starburst (purple) up to the center of the starburst. Then loop all the starburst bands counterclockwise, starting with the band that stretches from the center of the starburst to the lower right.

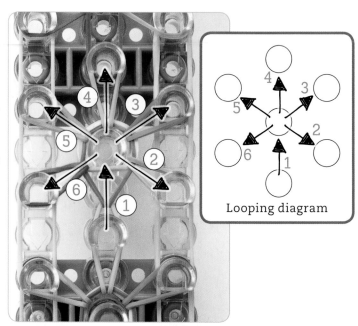

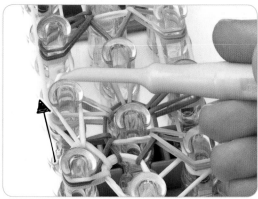

Looping diagram

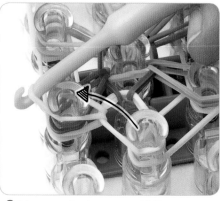

7 Repeat the pattern for the rest of the starbursts. Always remember to **push your hook down into the groove!**

8 Next, on the bottom middle peg, loop the second from bottom band **up through the groove** and onto the peg it came from, to the upper left. Make sure you hook the right band!

9 Hook the very bottom band on the peg you just looped to, and loop it to the peg immediately above it. Make sure to **push your hook down into the groove**. Repeat all the way up the column, looping each border band up to the peg above it.

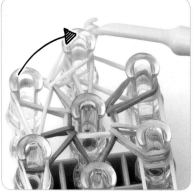

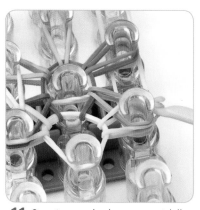

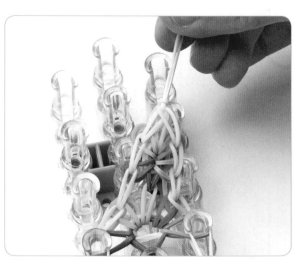

10 Loop the final band from the top left peg onto the top middle peg.

11 Starting at the bottom middle peg again, repeat the pattern (steps 8–10) to loop the entire right column, including looping the top right band to the top middle peg.

12 Secure the bands on the top peg with a slip knot (see page 16); you may want to extend the bracelet length with extra links (page 17). Pull the bracelet off the loom, and you're done!

34-Black (includes finishing band), 6-Red, 6-Neon Orange, 6-Yellow, 6-Lime Green, 6-Turquoise, 6-Purple

Star Rainbow: Try a black background for your next rainbow project! The colors shine way brighter than stars in the night sky, that's for sure!

34-Teal (includes finishing band), 18-Pink, 18-Neon Green

Pretty Peonies: This bracelet looks just like little flowers on the grass! By alternating the colors of the starbursts, you can create a really cool contrast.

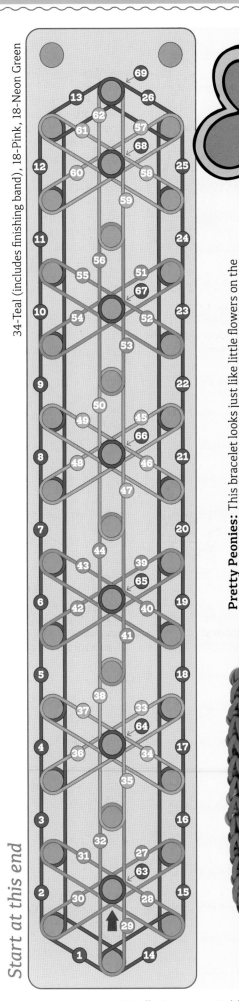

Flower Charm

This flower charm is small but adorable! The charm is so versatile: you can slide it onto a pencil to make a pencil topper, hang it from a bracelet as a charm, or even tie a bunch together for a bouquet! Have fun mastering this little beauty, and give them away as mini gifts.

Holiday Bloom   Pretty In Pink   Daisy

What You'll Need

7
Neon orange bands
(middle color 1)

6
Dark green bands
(outer petals)

6
Red bands
(middle color 2)

1
Neon orange
finishing band

Load It Up!

The **Load It Up!** pattern on the next page is shown in three layers to make it easy to follow. *Don't forget to add a double-looped band to the center of the star on the third layer.* (See Starburst Bracelet, page 35, for a brief explanation of this.)

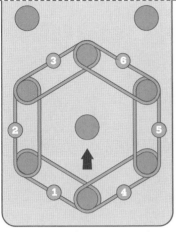

Layer 1 (middle color 1)

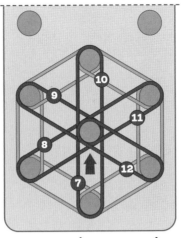

Layer 2 (middle color 2)

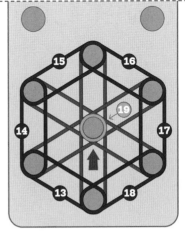

Layer 3 (outer petals)

These diagrams show the Rainbow Loom®, but if you are using a different loom, don't worry: follow the diagram and instructions exactly and your piece will turn out great. You may just have unused pegs.

Get Loopin'

1 Turn the loom so the arrow faces down. Push your hook down **into the groove** of the middle peg, into the loops formed by the double-looped band, and hook the top star band that is stretched from the center peg to the upper left peg. Loop it onto the upper left peg.

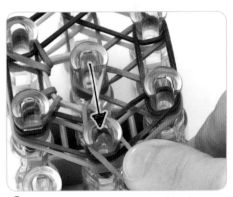

2 Loop the rest of the star bands like you did the first star band, moving counterclockwise. So, the next band goes to the bottom left peg. Make sure you **push your hook down into the groove** before you hook the band you want to loop. Make sure you loop the bands back onto the pegs they came from.

3 The third band of the star, which is stretched from the center peg to the bottom peg, is a tricky one to loop because it tries really hard to fall off the hook! You may want to use your fingers to loop it.

4 After you've finished looping the entire star, **push your hook down into** the bottom peg and hook the next-to-bottom band, which is the band that is stretched from the bottom peg to the peg to the upper left of it (like 7:00 on a clock face).

5 Loop the band onto the peg to the upper left of the bottom peg, which is the peg it came from. Make sure you looped the right band!

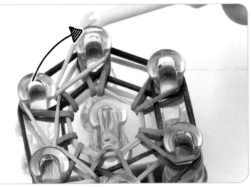

6 Hook and loop the two other bands on the left side of the hexagon, one at a time, to the pegs they came from. The first loops from the bottom left peg to the top left peg; the second loops from the top left peg to the top middle peg. Check to make sure your loom looks right.

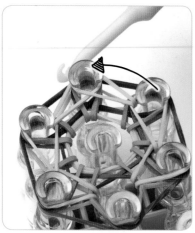

7 Hook and loop the right side of the shape the same way you did the left side, starting from the bottom peg (like steps 4–6).

8 Add a slip knot with your finishing band to the top middle peg to secure it, and pull the charm off the loom. (See page 16 for how to make a slip knot.) See how the petals are caught in the slip knot? We'll fix that now.

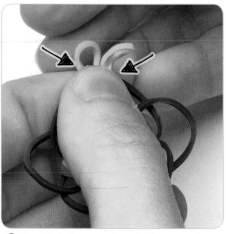

9 Carefully loosen the slip knot so that both loops of the slip knot separate, and hold both loops secure with one hand.

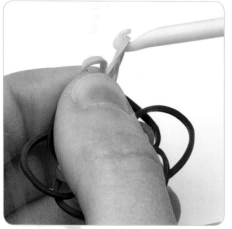

10 Now push your hook through the loop of the slip knot that is closest to you.

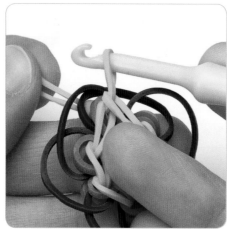

11 Hold the other slip knot loop, farthest from you, secure with your other hand.

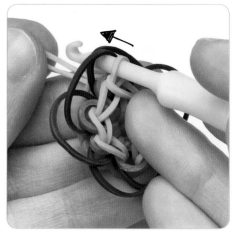

12 Slide the hook through the two adjacent outer petals, under where they cross, as shown.

13 Slide the hook through the far loop of the slip knot that you are holding onto.

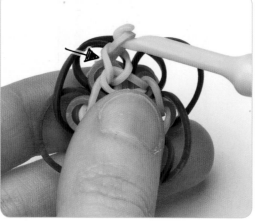

14 Get the far loop of the slip knot onto the very end of the hook and pull it back through the outer petals, then through the slip knot loop closest to you. The other slip knot loop will slide off the hook; that's okay.

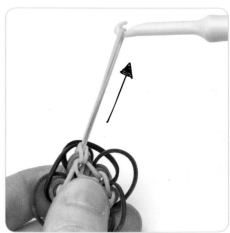

15 Pull the knot tight by pulling your hook. This makes a new slip knot, and you're done!

14-Fuchsia (includes finishing band), 6-Pink

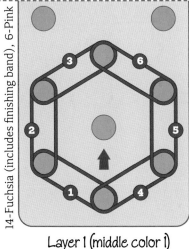

Layer 1 (middle color 1)

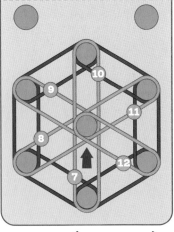

Layer 2 (middle color 2)

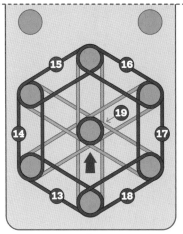

Layer 3 (outer petals)

Pretty In Pink: By making the outer petals the same color as some of the inside of the flower, you can create a nice mixed effect. Some real-life flowers have mixed colors just like this charm!

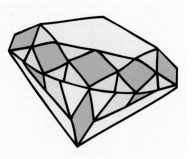

12-Yellow, 8-White (includes finishing band)

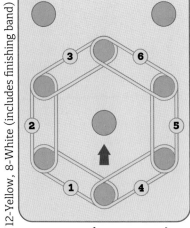

Layer 1 (middle color 1)

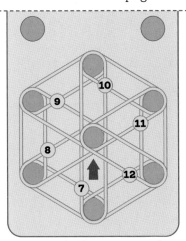

Layer 2 (middle color 2)

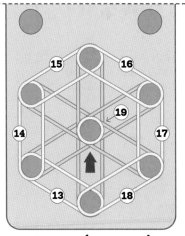

Layer 3 (outer petals)

Daisy: This daisy almost looks real! For this flower, only the outer petals are a different color; the inner bands are all yellow, to create a solid effect.

Dangly Earrings

These earrings keep their shape because they use double the bands! You can also make these earrings without using double bands (like Single Band Earrings, below). Another way to make these earrings is to make them with single bands, but only use 10 bands total instead of 17 (Mini Single Band Earrings).

Rainbow Wreath

Single Band Earrings

Mini Single Band Earrings

What You'll Need to Make Two Earrings

◯ **8** White bands	◯ **8** Ocean blue bands
◯ **12** Red bands	◯ **8** Lime green bands
◯ **8** Purple bands	◯ **8** Yellow bands

◯ **8** Neon orange bands	◯ **2** White finishing bands (1 per earring)
◯ **2** Black bands (extra bands that will be cut)	⌐ **2** French hook earring wires

Start at this end

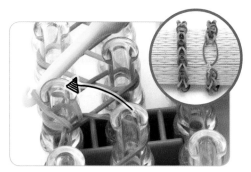

Load It Up!

Load your loom as if you were making a basic bracelet on the loom (page 9, steps 1–5), but place two bands on each pair of pegs instead of one. Place one at a time and do your best not to twist them together. For the last pair of pegs, just place one band. You're going to cut off this last band when you finish the earrings, so, if you want, make it the color you use the least.

Make the Earrings

1 To loop the bands, turn the loom upside down, then loop all the bands exactly as you would the basic bracelet (pages 10–11, steps 6–12), but grab both bands with the hook at once and loop them.

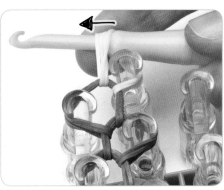

2 After looping the last pair of bands onto the top middle peg, push your hook all the way down through the loops on the top middle peg and pull the whole earring off the loom.

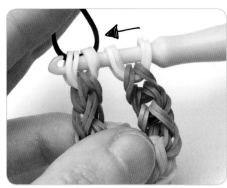

3 Making sure your earring isn't twisted, slide your hook through all four loops attached to the single band at the other end of the earring. Make sure you go in order; don't twist the four loops around.

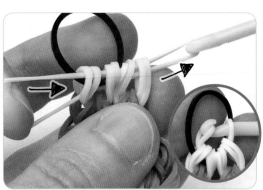

4 Hook and pull one end of a finishing band through all eight loops on your hook, then loop the other end up onto the hook, just like when you make a basic link on the hook (pages 14–15, steps 3–5). You can cut off the extra big loop band now.

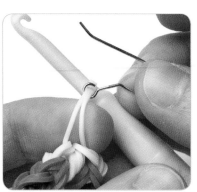

5 Slide both of the loops of the final link you just made onto the metal loop of the earring wire. Take the earring off your hook.

Hand and Foot Accessories

Be totally glamorous with a combination ring-and-bracelet or toe ring-and-anklet! These accessories only use basic links on the hook—no loom needed! Because everyone has different size hands and feet, you have to try the accessory on while you're making it to see how many bands works for you.

Rockin' Ring-and-Bracelet

What You'll Need

RING

◯ **10**
Orange bands

HAND CHAIN

◯ **9**
Pink bands

BRACELET

◯ **26**
Orange bands

 1
Clip

TOE RING

◯ **10**
Navy blue bands

FOOT CHAIN

◯ **9**
Turquoise bands

◯ **9**
Teal bands

ANKLET

◯ **34**
Navy blue bands

 1
Clip

Terrific Toe Ring-and-Anklet

Get Loopin'

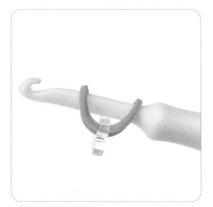

1 Start off the accessory by folding one band over your hook and clipping it with a clip to secure it temporarily.

2 Make a total of 10 basic links (as on pages 14–15), and loop the ring around your middle finger (or second toe) to check the fit. Once the ring is sized correctly, slide your hook through the two loops of the very first link, which you clipped.

3 Remove the clip, then make another basic link with the first band of your second color, sliding it through all four loops on the hook.

4 Make a total of 9 links with your second color—9 including the link that connects the ring. (If you're making the foot version, make a total of 18 links.) Put the ring on your finger (or toe) to check that the length is good.

5 Now make 13 basic links with your first color again. Then clip the last link you made. (For the foot version, make 17 links.) Put the ring on your finger (or toe) and wrap the links around your wrist (or foot) to check the fit.

6 Go back to the last of the chain links—the last one before you changed colors—and slide your hook through it.

7 Make 13 more basic links with your first color to create a separate strand of links that hangs beside the first set of 13 you made. (For the foot version, make 17 links.) (Match the number of links you make here to the number of links you decided on in step 5.)

8 Connect the last link you make to the last link of the first set by sliding the two loops of the last link onto the clip, for a total of four loops on the clip.

9 Put the accessory on and make any last changes to the size of the bracelet (or anklet). You're ready to step out in style!

Hippie Belt

Are you ready to make your biggest project yet? This accessory is sturdy and stylish at the same time. But it takes about 400 rubber bands to make, so make sure your stockpile is strong! Don't let the band count scare you. The technique isn't hard, it only uses the hook (no loom necessary), and everyone will ooh and ahh over your amazing creation. Peace, love, and rubber bands!

What You'll Need

- **50** Purple bands
- **50** Lime green bands
- **50** Caramel bands
- **50** Yellow bands
- **50** Fuchsia bands
- **160** Turquoise bands (for belt)
- **1** Clip

Get Loopin'

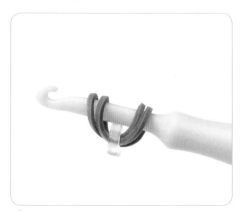

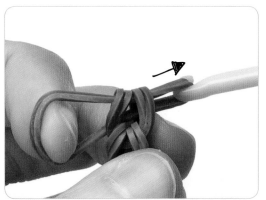

1 Fold two bands at once over the hook and clip them (the same as you did in step 1 for the Hand and Foot Accessories, page 45, but with two bands).

2 Make 25 basic links total (including the first link), but with double the bands: use two at a time, every time. You'll have to hold onto the bands more firmly than when you are just using one band, but it works just the same.

3 Once you've made 25 links, slide the loops of the first link (the link you clipped) onto the hook. Remove the clip.

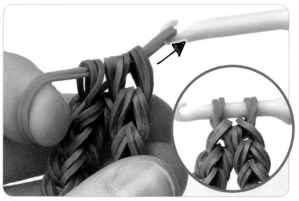

4 Pull two bands of the next color you want to use through all the bands on the hook and make a connecting link. This is like what you do to connect the ring in the Hand and Foot Accessories project (step 3, page 45).

5 Make 12 more links with double bands. Clip the last link on your hook and pull it off your hook.

6 Return to the first link of the new color, push your hook through it, and make 12 more links with double bands.

7 Slide the end of the first chain you finished onto the hook and remove the clip.

8 Make another connecting link with your next color as in step 4.

9 Keep repeating this pattern: make two halves of the circles, and then connect them (steps 5–8). Make a total of five connected circles.

10 After you make the fifth circle, make another connecting link as in step 8.

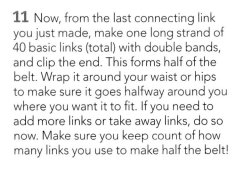

11 Now, from the last connecting link you just made, make one long strand of 40 basic links (total) with double bands, and clip the end. This forms half of the belt. Wrap it around your waist or hips to make sure it goes halfway around you where you want it to fit. If you need to add more links or take away links, do so now. Make sure you keep count of how many links you use to make half the belt!

12 Go back to the very first circle you made and push your hook through the center of the circle where you want the other half of the belt to connect.

13 Make a connecting link with double bands.

14 Make 40 total basic links with double bands, or the same total number you used in step 11.

15 Slide the end of the first half of the belt onto your hook. Take the clip off the end of the first half.

16 Make one last connecting link with two bands and clip it closed. You've just finished the grooviest belt ever!

Learn the Basics with the New EZ Looper™

The new EZ Looper™ by Pepperell Braiding Company is a round loom that makes it a cinch to make thick column patterns with rubber bands! You can make some of these patterns with full-sized looms, but the hollow design of the new loom makes it way easier and much faster. Plus, the small loom and hook slide easily into a pocket so you can take your tools anywhere!

To get started, you'll need just four simple items, most of which are available at your local craft or toy store.

You'll need:

> A small 6-peg round loom (such as the EZ Looper™)
> Small plastic clips
> Rubber bands (½" to ¾" in diameter)
> Small hook or crochet hook

The round loom works a bit differently than the full-sized loom. Each loom has 6 pegs arranged in a small circle. To make bracelets, rings, and all other kinds of cool accessories, you add layers of bands on top of one another, then loop the bottom layer of bands. You keep adding layers and looping layers, which builds a thick column of intertwined rubber bands instead of a flat row of rubber bands like the full-sized loom creates.

One of the coolest things about the round loom is that with just one loom, you can make any design as long as you want! Just keep adding layers and looping.

Before You Begin...

Mark the top of one of the pegs with nail polish, paint, white out, or marker. This will help you keep track of what you're doing for every design you make!

There are so many cool designs you can make with the round loom! This one uses four pegs and an alternating pattern of layers of bands. Learn how to make the basic bracelet with the round loom on page 50, make a more advanced bracelet on page 52, and check out other cool design ideas on page 56!

Making the Basic Bracelet on a Round Loom

Making a basic design for a bracelet on a round loom is just a matter of seconds! Once you understand how to make this design, all the more complicated designs will be easy to make.

What You'll Need

› 25 rubber bands (for this example, 13 orange and 12 navy blue)
› 1 clip
› Round loom
› Hook

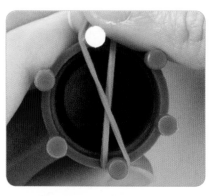

1 Turn your loom so the marked peg is at the top. Place the first band, crossed in a figure eight as shown, from the marked peg to the peg below it.

2 Place the second band on top of the first band, not crossed.

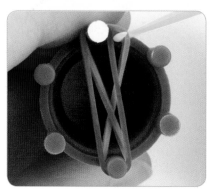

3 Hook the bottom band on the marked peg from the side as shown.

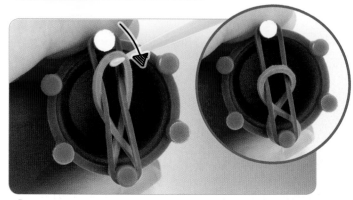

4 Loop the band up and over the peg, from the outside to the inside, so that it lies loose in the middle.

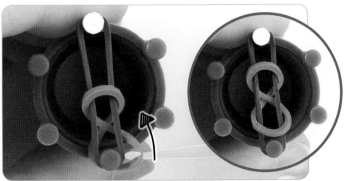

6 Push the bands down in the center of the loom with your finger. Always push the bands down after every completed looping, because this makes room at the top of the pegs for you to add the next set of bands.

5 Hook and loop the bottom band on the other peg the same way.

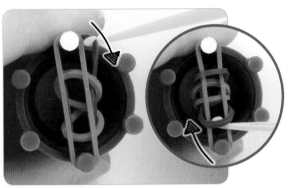

9 Keep adding one new band and then looping the bottom band until you run out of bands or reach the desired length. The links will hang out of the bottom of the loom.

7 Place another band on top of the bands, on the same two pegs.

8 Hook and loop the new bottom band on both pegs the same way as you did the first band in steps 4–6.

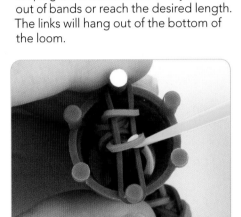

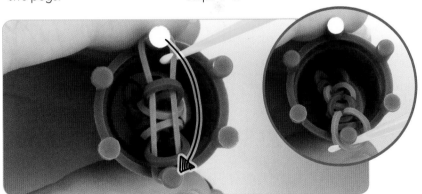

10 To finish the bracelet, after hooking your last bottom band, start by hooking the only band left on the marked peg from the outside as shown. Lift the band off the peg and fold it down to loop it around the bottom peg.

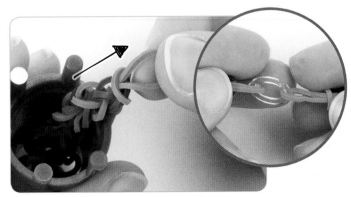

11 Hook and loop the bottom band up and over the peg from the outside to the inside, then pull the remaining band on the peg tight to secure the knot you just created.

12 Lift the band off the peg, pull your bracelet out of the loom, add a clip, and you're done!

Simple Four-Peg Bracelet

This design uses layers of two bands on four pegs. It's very easy to do, and makes a nifty round bracelet. Just keep repeating the pattern!

True Blue Stripes   Party Mix   Tech Stripes   Color Blocks

What You'll Need

25 Turquoise bands

25 Navy blue bands

1 Clip

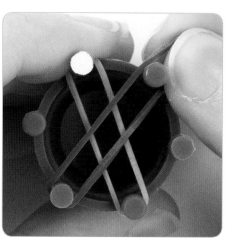

1 Turn your loom so the marked peg is at the top. Place two bands as shown.

2 Place two additional bands the same way to make an identical second layer on top of the first.

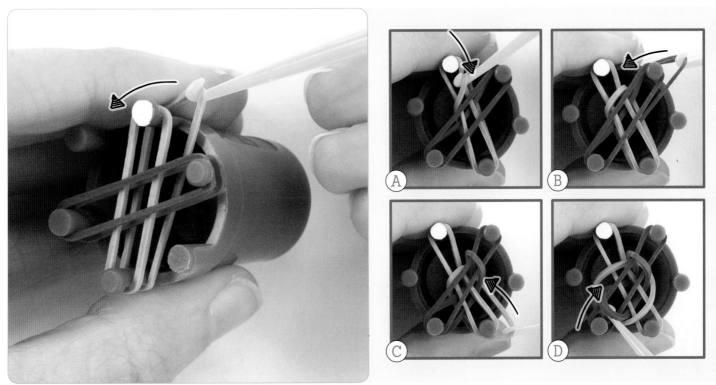

3 Hook the bottom band on the marked peg, then loop it up and over the peg from the outside to the inside (A). Going clockwise, hook and loop the bottom band on all four pegs this way (B, C, and D).

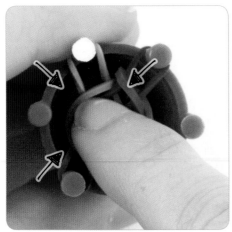

4 After looping all four bottom bands, push the bands down in the center of the loom with your finger.

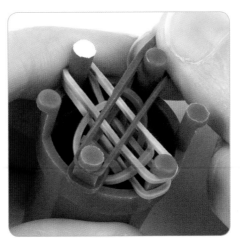

5 Now place two additional bands the same way again to make another layer, as you did in step 2.

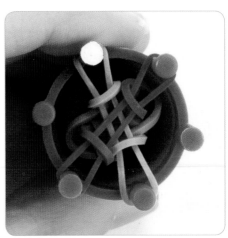

6 Loop the bottom layer just as you did before, and push down in the center. Your loom will look like this.

7 Repeat this pattern of placing bands and looping until you reach the desired length. When you are ready to stop, loop the bottom layer of bands so that there is only one band on each peg, but don't add another layer of bands.

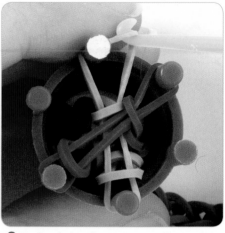

8 To finish the design, you will create a knot with one rubber band. Start by hooking the band on the marked peg.

9 Then, transfer the band you hooked onto the next peg clockwise that has a band on it.

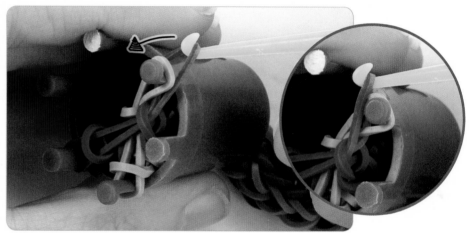

10 Hook the bottom band on the peg you just moved to, and loop it up and over the peg from the outside to the inside.

11 Hook the remaining band on the peg and transfer it onto the next peg clockwise that has a band on it, just as you did in step 9.

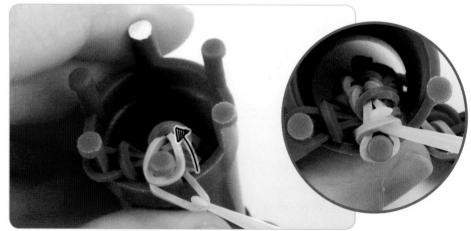

12 Hook the bottom band on the peg you just moved to, and loop it up and over the peg from the outside to the inside, just as you did in step 10.

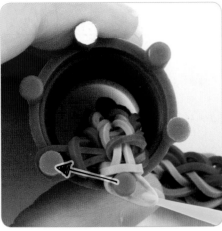

13 Hook the remaining band on the peg and transfer it onto the next peg clockwise that has a band on it, just as you did in steps 9 and 11.

14 Hook the bottom band on the peg you just moved to, and loop it up and over the peg from the outside to the inside, just as you did in steps 10 and 12.

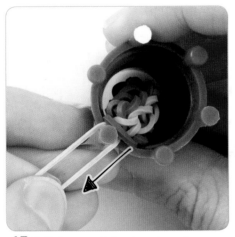
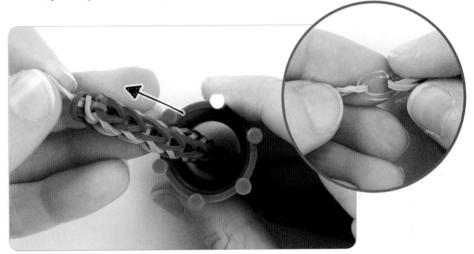

15 Pull the remaining band on the peg tight to secure the knot you just created.

16 Lift the band off the peg, pull your bracelet out of the loom, add a clip, and you're done!

Color Ideas

Color Blocks: To create thick blocks of color, use one color per layer for five layers, then switch to a different color.

Party Mix: To create an alternating pattern, use the same two colors for the whole bracelet, but switch which peg you put them on for every layer. For the red and yellow bracelet, for example, for the first layer place red then yellow, for the second layer place yellow then red, and keep alternating like that.

Tech Stripes: To create cool switched-up stripes, do five layers with two colors, then five layers with the same colors but on switched pegs. For the green and black bracelet, for example, do five layers first placing green then black, then do five layers first placing black then green.

Round Loom Ideas!

Shown here are just some of the interesting and fun new designs you can make with a round loom. The way different bracelets look depends on how many pegs you use and how many bands you place and loop at a time. Experiment with patterns, colors, and lengths, and have fun with the new loom!

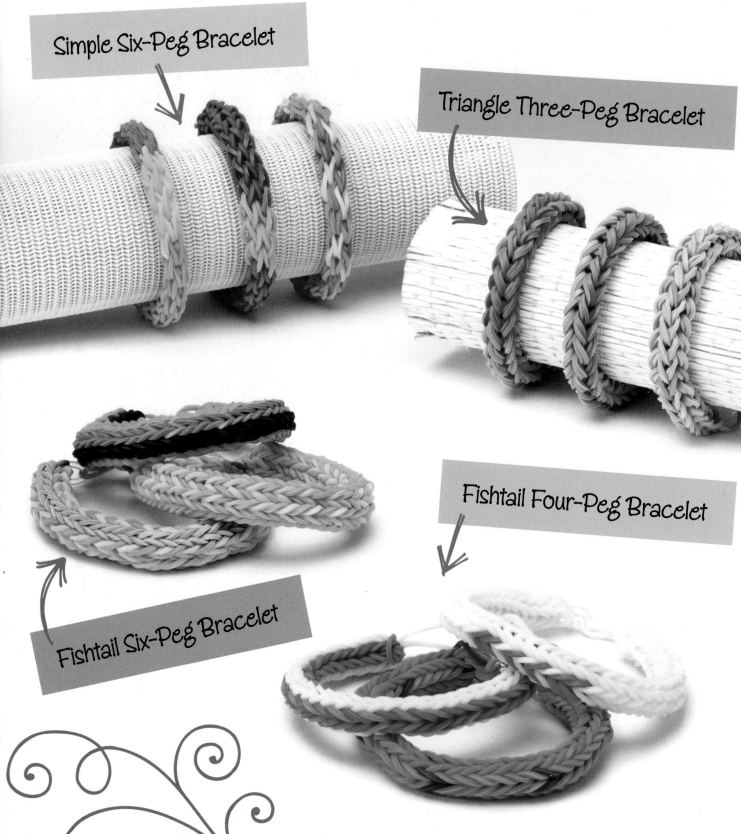

Simple Six-Peg Bracelet

Triangle Three-Peg Bracelet

Fishtail Four-Peg Bracelet

Fishtail Six-Peg Bracelet